CYBER EXTORTION

A Comprehensive Guide to Ransomware

By

Hassam Ali K

This is a work of fiction. Names, characters, places, and incidents are products of the author's imagination or are used fictitiously. Any resemblance to actual persons, living or dead, events, or locales is entirely coincidental.

HAK CONSULTANCY SERVICES

Published by **HAK Consultancy Services**

For permissions or inquiries, contact:

hakconsultancy@outlook.com

Table of Contents

INTRODUCTION
Cybersecurity Threats

In the 21st century, as our reliance on technology grows, so do the threats that accompany it. The internet has revolutionized communication, commerce, healthcare, and nearly every facet of modern life. However, this vast digital network is also a playground for cybercriminals who exploit vulnerabilities to cause harm. From stealing personal information to halting the operations of critical infrastructure, the impact of cyberattacks can be devastating.

One of the most notorious forms of cybercrime today is **ransomware**. This type of malware has evolved into a global problem, targeting individuals, corporations, and even governments. It locks users out of their own files, demanding a ransom for their release. The costs of these attacks—both financial and personal—can be immense.

But ransomware is not alone in this battle for control over our digital world. Worms, trojans, spyware, and other forms of malware constantly threaten our online safety. To navigate this dangerous landscape, it's essential to understand the nature of these threats, how they operate, and the steps we can take to protect ourselves.

In this book, we will explore ransomware in depth, but we will also dive into other types of viruses and malware. We will provide practical advice on how to avoid falling victim to these attacks and what to do if your system becomes compromised. By the end, you will have a clear understanding of the cyber threats that surround us and how to stay safe in the digital age.

CHAPTER 1
What is Ransomware?

Ransomware is a type of malicious software, or malware, that infects a computer system and locks down files or devices until the user pays a ransom to the attacker. The ransom, typically demanded in cryptocurrency, promises to release the data or unlock the system. While the earliest forms of ransomware date back to the late 1980s, it wasn't until the mid-2000s that ransomware emerged as a widespread threat. Today, it is one of the most dangerous and costly types of cyberattacks.

Ransomware has evolved significantly over the years. Early attacks were often rudimentary, but modern versions use sophisticated encryption techniques that make it almost impossible for victims to recover their data without paying. Additionally, as ransomware became more profitable, cybercriminals began targeting larger organizations with deeper pockets, such as corporations, hospitals, and government agencies.

The rise of **cryptocurrencies** like Bitcoin has only fueled the growth of ransomware. These digital currencies allow attackers to collect payments anonymously, making it harder for authorities to track down the criminals behind the attacks.

TYPES OF RANSOMWARES

There are several distinct types of ransomwares, each with its own methods of attack and ransom demands:

1. **Locker Ransomware:** Locker ransomware completely locks victims out of their devices. The infected system becomes unusable, often with a full-screen ransom message displayed, demanding payment to regain access. While this type of ransomware doesn't typically encrypt individual files, it still causes major disruption, especially if the targeted device is critical for work or communication.
2. **Crypto Ransomware:** Crypto ransomware takes a more insidious approach. Instead of locking users out of their entire system, it encrypts specific files and folders, rendering them unreadable without the correct decryption key. These files could include photos, videos, documents, spreadsheets, and more—often targeting the most valuable data on the device.

   The ransomware typically displays a countdown timer, adding psychological pressure on the victim to pay quickly. Crypto ransomware is particularly harmful because, even if the infected system is fixed, the data remains inaccessible without the decryption key.

3. **Doxware (Leakware):** Doxware, or leakware, is a variant of ransomware that takes a personal approach to extortion. Instead of simply encrypting files, it threatens to release or "leak" sensitive personal information, such as private photos, financial data, or confidential business records, unless the victim pays. This can lead to a loss of privacy and even legal issues for the victim, particularly for businesses handling confidential client data.

How Ransomware Works: The Lifecycle of an Attack

Ransomware attacks typically follow a well-defined process, and understanding these steps can help both individuals and organizations recognize and defend against them:

1. **Infection (Entry Point)**: The ransomware gains entry to a system through various methods, the most common being:

   - **Phishing Emails**: Cybercriminals often send emails that appear legitimate, encouraging the recipient to click on a link or download an attachment. These attachments or links install the ransomware onto the system once opened.

- **Exploiting Software Vulnerabilities**: Outdated software or operating systems often have security weaknesses that cybercriminals exploit to gain access to a network.

- **Drive-by Downloads**: Ransomware can be delivered simply by visiting a compromised website, where malicious code is automatically downloaded to the victim's system.

2. **Execution and Encryption**: Once inside the system, the ransomware launches itself, scanning for valuable files such as documents, spreadsheets, photos, and more. It uses sophisticated encryption algorithms (such as RSA or AES) to lock these files, making them unreadable to the victim without a unique decryption key. This encryption process can happen in the background, often unnoticed until the victim tries to access their files.

3. **Ransom Demand**: After the files are encrypted, a ransom note appears on the victim's screen, explaining the situation. The note typically includes details about how to pay the ransom, usually via cryptocurrency like Bitcoin, and warns that the price will increase or the files will be deleted if the ransom is not paid within a certain timeframe. Some ransom notes include detailed instructions on how to purchase and transfer cryptocurrency for victims unfamiliar with it.

WHY IS RANSOMWARE SO DANGEROUS?

Ransomware is particularly dangerous for several reasons:

1. **Data Loss**: If the ransom is not paid, victims may lose their critical data forever. In many cases, attackers do not provide the decryption key even after payment, leaving victims without their files and out of pocket.
2. **Financial Loss**: Paying the ransom can be expensive, often costing individuals hundreds of dollars and organizations millions. However, there's no guarantee that paying will result in file recovery, which adds to the financial burden of the attack.
3. **Operational Disruption**: Ransomware can bring an entire business to a halt. Hospitals have had to divert emergency patients, businesses have been unable to operate, and governments have been forced to shut down services, all due to ransomware attacks.
4. **Reputational Damage**: For organizations, being a victim of ransomware can severely damage public trust. If sensitive data is stolen or leaked, it can lead to legal and regulatory consequences, further amplifying the harm caused.

CHAPTER 2
The Ransomware Ecosystem

Ransomware is not just a simple attack; it's part of a broader, highly organized cybercrime ecosystem. Understanding how ransomware spreads, how attackers operate, and the tools they use will give you a deeper insight into its effectiveness and persistence.

This chapter will explore the key components that make up the ransomware ecosystem, including the various attack vectors, the role of encryption technology, and how cryptocurrencies facilitate these attacks.

ATTACK VECTORS: HOW RANSOMWARE INFECTS SYSTEMS

Ransomware doesn't just appear out of nowhere—it has to enter your system through an "attack vector." An attack vector is the path or method by which a hacker gains access to your computer or network. The most common attack vectors used by ransomware attackers include:

Phishing Emails

One of the most effective and widely used attack vectors is phishing. Phishing emails are designed to trick users into downloading malicious attachments or clicking on links that lead to websites that automatically infect their system with ransomware.

Phishing emails are typically disguised as legitimate communications from trusted sources such as banks, online services, or even coworkers. These emails often contain a sense of urgency, such as "Your account has been compromised" or "You have an overdue invoice," prompting the recipient to open a file or click a link.

Once clicked, the malware is downloaded onto the user's system, where it can silently encrypt files or lock the entire system.

Malicious Downloads

Malicious downloads can occur when users download seemingly harmless files from untrustworthy websites. These files might appear to be software updates, free programs, or multimedia content but are actually bundled with ransomware. This is known as a "drive-by download," where malware is installed on a system without the user's knowledge.

Exploiting Software Vulnerabilities

Outdated software is another significant entry point for ransomware. Many software programs, including operating systems and applications, have vulnerabilities that can be exploited by attackers. When security patches are not applied promptly, these vulnerabilities can be used to deliver ransomware payloads without any user interaction.

In 2017, the **WannaCry ransomware** attack exploited a known vulnerability in Microsoft Windows that had not been patched in many systems, leading to one of the largest ransomware outbreaks in history. It affected over 200,000 computers across the globe, demonstrating the critical importance of keeping systems up to date.

Remote Desktop Protocol (RDP)

Remote Desktop Protocol (RDP) allows users to remotely control their computer or network over the internet. However, poorly secured RDP sessions are a major target for ransomware attackers. Cybercriminals often use brute force attacks to guess RDP credentials or buy stolen credentials from underground markets.

Once they gain access, they can manually deploy ransomware across the network, locking down systems and demanding ransom from multiple victims within the organization.

The Role of Encryption in Ransomware

At the heart of ransomware lies encryption—a process that scrambles data in such a way that it becomes unreadable without the correct decryption key. Encryption is a legitimate technology used by millions of people to protect sensitive data, but cybercriminals have weaponized it to extort victims.

When ransomware encrypts files, it uses strong encryption algorithms like AES (Advanced Encryption Standard) or RSA (Rivest–Shamir–Adleman). These algorithms are nearly impossible to break using brute force methods without the correct key, making it extremely difficult for victims to recover their data on their own.

Symmetric Encryption (AES)

AES is a symmetric encryption algorithm, meaning the same key is used for both encryption and decryption. Ransomware using AES encrypts the victim's files with a single key. However, this key is typically stored on the attacker's remote server, making it inaccessible to the victim unless the ransom is paid.

Asymmetric Encryption (RSA)

RSA is an asymmetric encryption algorithm, using two different keys: a public key and a private key. The public key is used to encrypt the data, while the private key is needed to decrypt it. In ransomware attacks that use RSA, the public key is embedded within the ransomware and encrypts the victim's files, but the private key (needed for decryption) is held by the attacker.

Attackers often combine AES and RSA encryption to speed up the process while maintaining a high level of security. First, they use AES to encrypt the files and then encrypt the AES key using RSA, making it impossible to decrypt the files without both keys.

The Role of Cryptocurrencies in Ransomware Attacks

One of the reasons ransomware has become so successful in recent years is the rise of **cryptocurrencies**, such as Bitcoin. Cryptocurrencies allow attackers to collect ransom payments anonymously, making it difficult for authorities to trace the transactions back to the criminals.

Before the advent of Bitcoin and other cryptocurrencies, attackers faced a significant challenge: how to collect ransom payments without getting caught. Traditional payment methods like bank transfers or credit cards left trails that could be easily tracked. Cryptocurrencies changed this by providing a level of anonymity not available in conventional financial systems.

Why Bitcoin?

Bitcoin is the most popular cryptocurrency used in ransomware attacks due to its widespread adoption and the relative ease of using it. Unlike traditional currencies, Bitcoin transactions do not require personal information, making it difficult to track down who made or received a payment. While Bitcoin transactions are visible on the blockchain, the identity behind the wallet addresses is hidden, providing a layer of anonymity.

Cryptocurrency Wallets and Payment Demands

Attackers often create multiple cryptocurrency wallets for each victim, further obscuring their identity. Once a payment is made, they transfer the funds to other wallets, "mix" them through services that aggregate and redistribute funds (making tracking harder), and eventually cash out through cryptocurrency exchanges.

Alternatives to Bitcoin

While Bitcoin is the most commonly used cryptocurrency in ransomware attacks, others like **Monero** and **Zcash** are becoming popular due to their increased privacy features. These cryptocurrencies are designed to provide enhanced anonymity, making it even harder for law enforcement agencies to trace payments.

The Ransomware-as-a-Service (RaaS) Model

One of the most dangerous trends in the ransomware ecosystem is the rise of **Ransomware-as-a-Service (RaaS)**. Just like legitimate businesses offer software services through the cloud, cybercriminals are now offering ransomware as a service to other criminals.

In the RaaS model, the developers of ransomware create the malware and provide it to "affiliates" who are responsible for spreading the infection. In return, the developers take a percentage of the ransom payments made by victims, while the affiliates pocket the rest. This business model has dramatically lowered the barrier to entry for cybercriminals, allowing even those with little technical knowledge to launch ransomware attacks.

Affiliate Programs

In the RaaS model, affiliates don't need to develop ransomware themselves. Instead, they purchase access to ransomware kits or partner with established criminal groups. These affiliates are responsible for finding victims, launching the attack, and collecting the ransom, while the creators handle the backend operations.

Profit Sharing

Once an affiliate successfully collects a ransom payment, a portion of the funds goes to the ransomware developers. This profit-sharing model has helped ransomware spread rapidly, as affiliates are incentivized to target a broad range of victims.

The Cybercrime Underground

Ransomware is part of a larger underground economy that includes a wide variety of illegal goods and services. This ecosystem is supported by dark web marketplaces where hackers can buy and sell malicious software, stolen data, and even hire other cybercriminals to carry out attacks.

Dark Web Markets

The dark web is a part of the internet that is not indexed by search engines and is accessible only through special software, such as the Tor browser. It is here that cybercriminals buy and sell ransomware kits, stolen data, hacking tools, and other illicit goods. The anonymity of the dark web provides a haven for criminals to operate without fear of being caught.

Stolen Data for Sale

Ransomware attacks are often paired with data theft. Attackers not only lock down a victim's files but also exfiltrate sensitive data, which they then sell on the dark web. This data can include personal information, financial records, or intellectual property, creating a secondary revenue stream for cybercriminals.

CHAPTER 3
Types of Ransomware

Ransomware, despite having a singular goal of extorting victims for money, comes in many different forms. Each type of ransomware employs distinct methods to infect systems and hold data hostage. While they all cause damage, understanding the nuances of each variant can help individuals and organizations better prepare for and mitigate these threats. This chapter delves into the major types of ransomware that have emerged over the years, each with its unique tactics and consequences.

Locker Ransomware: The System Blockade

Locker ransomware is one of the more straightforward forms of ransomware. It doesn't encrypt individual files but instead locks the victim out of their entire device. Once a computer or mobile phone is infected, the user is unable to access any part of their system until a ransom is paid. A full-screen message often takes over the display, notifying the victim of the attack and providing instructions on how to pay the ransom.

While this type of ransomware might seem less severe since it doesn't destroy files, it still causes significant disruption. Victims lose access to everything on their device until they meet the attackers' demands. For businesses, the inability to use critical systems can grind operations to a halt, leading to missed deadlines, financial losses, and reputational damage. For individuals, the loss of access to personal devices can be equally distressing, especially if the infected device contains important information.

Locker ransomware usually targets lower-level operating system functionality, making it difficult for even tech-savvy users to bypass the lock without paying the ransom. Unlike crypto ransomware, which uses encryption to render files unreadable, locker ransomware focuses on holding the system itself hostage, denying access entirely.

Crypto Ransomware: Encrypting Your Data

Crypto ransomware is perhaps the most well-known and dangerous form of ransomware. Instead of blocking access to an entire system, this type encrypts specific files and folders, making them unusable without a decryption key. Files such as documents, spreadsheets, photos, and videos—often the most valuable data on a system—are targeted by the attackers. The victim is then presented with a ransom note demanding payment in exchange for the decryption key.

This type of ransomware has become increasingly sophisticated over the years. Early versions of crypto ransomware used relatively weak encryption algorithms, which security researchers could sometimes break. However, modern versions employ strong encryption standards such as AES (Advanced Encryption Standard) and RSA (Rivest–Shamir–Adleman), making it nearly impossible to recover the encrypted data without the decryption key.

The psychological pressure applied by crypto ransomware is immense. Victims often face a countdown timer, which threatens to increase the ransom amount or delete the decryption key entirely if payment is not made within a certain timeframe. This sense of urgency often pushes victims to pay quickly, sometimes without exploring alternative options for data recovery.

The financial cost of crypto ransomware can be staggering, especially for organizations. In some cases, businesses have had to pay millions of dollars to recover their files, and yet, there's no guarantee that paying the ransom will result in file recovery. Some victims never receive the promised decryption key, or they find that the data has been damaged during the encryption process.

DOXWARE (LEAKWARE): EXTORTION ON A PERSONAL LEVEL

Doxware, also known as leakware, adds an extra layer of extortion by threatening to release the victim's sensitive data publicly. Unlike other types of ransomware that primarily focus on locking files or systems, doxware capitalizes on the fear of exposure. If the ransom is not paid, the attacker threatens to leak private photos, financial records, business contracts, or other confidential information to the public or competitors.

The threat of public exposure can be devastating for both individuals and businesses. Personal data, such as private photographs or medical records, could be shared with the victim's social network or posted publicly. For businesses, confidential information like client details, financial data, or intellectual property might be sold to competitors or published online, leading to reputational damage and legal consequences.

Doxware is particularly effective against high-profile targets like corporations, celebrities, and politicians. Even if victims are able to recover their files, the mere possibility of having their sensitive information exposed can be enough to compel them to pay the ransom.

Ransomware with Double Extortion: The New Threat Landscape

In recent years, a more dangerous form of ransomware has emerged: double extortion ransomware. In these attacks, cybercriminals not only encrypt the victim's files but also exfiltrate sensitive data before deploying the ransomware. Once the data is encrypted, the attackers demand a ransom for the decryption key. However, if the victim refuses to pay, the attackers threaten to leak the stolen data to the public or sell it on the dark web.

Double extortion ransomware is especially effective because it amplifies the pressure on the victim. Even if a company has reliable backups and can restore its data without paying the ransom, the threat of having proprietary information leaked can push them to pay. The fear of data breaches, regulatory fines, and reputational damage looms large in these scenarios, making double extortion one of the most successful ransomware strategies today.

The **Maze** ransomware group was one of the first to adopt this technique, setting a precedent for other cybercriminals. Many other groups have followed suit, making double extortion attacks a growing concern for both private individuals and large organizations.

RANSOMWARE TARGETING SPECIFIC INDUSTRIES

While ransomware can affect anyone with a vulnerable device, some sectors are more heavily targeted due to the nature of their data and operations. Healthcare, finance, education, and government agencies have become prime targets for ransomware attacks.

Healthcare: The healthcare sector has become a major target for ransomware attacks. Hospitals and healthcare providers handle vast amounts of sensitive personal data, including medical records and insurance details. The critical nature of their operations—where downtime can literally cost lives—makes them more likely to pay a ransom to quickly restore access to their systems. Attacks like the infamous **WannaCry** ransomware in 2017, which impacted the UK's National Health Service (NHS), highlighted the vulnerability of healthcare systems to cyberattacks.

Finance: Banks and financial institutions are also highly targeted due to the valuable data they hold. The financial industry is seen as a lucrative target, as organizations are often willing to pay hefty ransoms to avoid the regulatory fallout, customer dissatisfaction, and legal consequences of compromised data.

Education: Schools and universities, which often operate with tight budgets and outdated systems, have become another frequent target of ransomware. These institutions hold a large amount of personal data related to students, faculty, and research. However, they often lack the cybersecurity infrastructure needed to defend against attacks, making them an easy target for cybercriminals.

Government: Government agencies, especially local governments, are also prime targets. These entities often rely on legacy systems that are outdated and poorly maintained, making them vulnerable to ransomware. Additionally, government systems are critical to public safety and daily operations, meaning that downtime can result in chaos and pressure to pay the ransom quickly.

Mobile Ransomware: Targeting Smartphones

While most ransomware attacks focus on desktops and servers, mobile ransomware has been on the rise, targeting both Android and iOS devices. Mobile ransomware functions similarly to its desktop counterpart, either locking the device or encrypting files until the victim pays the ransom.

The rapid growth of mobile ransomware is due to the increasing amount of personal and financial data stored on smartphones. With users often neglecting to install security updates or use antivirus software on their mobile devices, these attacks have become more common. Android devices, in particular, are more susceptible to mobile ransomware due to their open ecosystem, which allows users to install apps from unofficial sources.

Mobile ransomware can be particularly damaging, as many users rely on their smartphones for banking, communication, and access to personal accounts. Losing access to these devices can have a significant impact on their daily lives.

CHAPTER 4
Defending Against Ransomware

As ransomware continues to evolve, the importance of understanding how to defend against these attacks becomes paramount. Prevention, detection, and response strategies are essential components of a strong defense against ransomware. In this chapter, we will explore these methods in depth, focusing on best practices that individuals, businesses, and institutions can adopt to minimize the risk of infection and mitigate the impact of an attack.

THE IMPORTANCE OF A PROACTIVE DEFENSE

In the fight against ransomware, the best offense is a strong defense. Cybersecurity experts agree that being proactive—rather than reactive—is key to protecting against ransomware. The first step to proactive defense is education. Understanding how ransomware spreads and the potential vulnerabilities in your system will allow you to take appropriate measures to reduce your exposure to these attacks.

For individuals, this might mean learning to recognize phishing emails and ensuring that security software is up-to-date. For businesses, it requires a comprehensive approach that involves securing networks, training employees, and implementing data backup solutions. Governments and critical industries must also develop response plans that ensure services remain operational in the event of an attack. Regardless of the specific strategies employed, the cornerstone of ransomware defense is preparedness.

KEEPING SYSTEMS UPDATED

One of the simplest yet most effective methods to defend against ransomware is keeping software and systems updated. Many ransomware attacks exploit vulnerabilities in outdated operating systems, applications, and security software. These vulnerabilities, once discovered by cybercriminals, provide an open door to infect systems with ransomware.

The **WannaCry** ransomware attack in 2017 is a prime example of how unpatched vulnerabilities can lead to massive damage. This attack exploited a flaw in Microsoft Windows that had been patched months before the attack began. However, many organizations and individuals had not applied the security update, leaving their systems exposed.

To mitigate this risk, ensure that all software, including operating systems, antivirus programs, and other applications, are set to update automatically. In corporate environments, IT teams should regularly monitor systems for patches and updates, prioritizing those that address known security vulnerabilities.

Backing Up Your Data: The Last Line of Defense

Even with the best security measures in place, no system is entirely immune to ransomware. This is why backing up data is an essential component of any ransomware defense strategy. A reliable and up-to-date backup ensures that even if ransomware strikes, you can restore your files without paying the ransom.

When implementing a backup strategy, it is crucial to follow the **3-2-1 rule**:

- Keep three copies of your data: one primary and two backups.

- Store the backups on two different types of media (for example, an external hard drive and cloud storage).
- Ensure that one of the backups is stored offsite or offline, disconnected from your main network.

Having an offline backup is particularly important because many ransomware variants are designed to seek out and encrypt any backups connected to the infected system. An offline backup—one that is not accessible through the network—remains safe from ransomware, allowing you to restore your data even in the worst-case scenario.

Cloud services also offer a secure backup option, provided that they implement strong encryption and access controls. Many cloud providers offer automatic backup features, ensuring that your data is regularly saved without requiring manual intervention.

Training and Awareness: The Human Factor

No matter how advanced a system's defenses may be, human error remains one of the most common reasons ransomware attacks succeed. Phishing emails, malicious attachments, and fraudulent websites all rely on the victim's interaction to deliver the ransomware payload. This is why educating users—whether employees in an organization or family members at home—is critical.

For businesses, training programs should focus on how to recognize phishing emails, suspicious attachments, and deceptive links. Employees should be encouraged to scrutinize unexpected emails, even if they appear to come from a trusted source. If an email contains an attachment or a link, users should confirm its legitimacy before clicking. Simple practices, such as hovering over a link to check its URL or verifying email addresses for slight misspellings, can prevent ransomware from gaining a foothold.

Cybersecurity awareness training should also include simulations of phishing attacks to test employees' ability to recognize threats in real time. Many organizations now use simulated phishing campaigns as part of their regular training programs to ensure employees remain vigilant.

For individuals, being cautious with unsolicited emails, attachments, and downloads is equally important. If something seems too good to be true, such as a free offer or a message claiming you've won a prize, it's best to ignore it. Additionally, downloading software only from trusted sources and websites can significantly reduce the risk of infection.

Antivirus and Anti-Ransomware Tools

Modern antivirus software has evolved to include anti-ransomware features designed to detect and block ransomware before it can execute its malicious activities. These tools rely on signature-based detection, behavioral analysis, and real-time scanning to identify and neutralize ransomware threats.

Signature-based detection compares files against a database of known malware signatures. While this method is effective for identifying previously known ransomware variants, it may struggle to detect new or modified strains that have not yet been cataloged. To address this limitation, many security solutions incorporate behavioral analysis, which monitors files for suspicious actions (such as unauthorized encryption of data) and blocks them if they match known ransomware behavior.

Some security products now offer specialized anti-ransomware tools that are designed specifically to stop ransomware in its tracks. These tools monitor file changes and flag unauthorized attempts to encrypt files, preventing ransomware from completing its attack. For businesses, endpoint detection and response (EDR) solutions are often employed to protect against ransomware across multiple devices within a network.

Although antivirus and anti-ransomware tools can provide an additional layer of security, they are not foolproof. New strains of ransomware are constantly being developed, and attackers are finding ways to bypass even the most sophisticated defenses. For this reason, antivirus software should be seen as one component of a broader defense strategy, not a silver bullet.

Network Security: Protecting the Digital Perimeter

Securing a network is crucial to preventing ransomware from spreading within an organization. Once inside a network, ransomware can quickly move laterally, infecting multiple systems and potentially taking down entire operations. Strong network security practices, such as segmenting networks, using firewalls, and monitoring traffic, are vital to containing ransomware infections.

Network segmentation involves dividing a network into smaller, isolated segments. If one segment is compromised, the ransomware is confined to that area and cannot spread to other parts of the network. For example, an organization might separate its financial systems from its customer data systems to prevent a breach in one area from affecting the other.

Firewalls and intrusion detection systems (IDS) can help block malicious traffic and prevent unauthorized access to a network. Firewalls monitor incoming and outgoing network traffic and enforce rules to allow or block specific traffic based on security policies. An IDS, on the other hand, scans network activity for suspicious behavior and alerts administrators if an anomaly is detected.

Additionally, network monitoring tools can help identify unusual patterns that may indicate a ransomware attack in progress. For example, a sudden spike in file encryption or outbound connections to unfamiliar servers might be a sign that ransomware has entered the network. By monitoring network activity in real time, administrators can quickly isolate infected machines and contain the damage.

Incident Response: Reacting to a Ransomware Attack

Despite all preventive measures, it is still possible to fall victim to a ransomware attack. When this happens, having a well-prepared incident response plan can make the difference between a quick recovery and a prolonged crisis.

An incident response plan should outline the steps to take if ransomware is detected, including isolating infected systems, notifying relevant stakeholders, and restoring from backups. The goal of incident response is to minimize the damage, stop the spread of the malware, and recover data as quickly as possible.

One of the first steps in an incident response plan is to disconnect infected systems from the network to prevent the ransomware from spreading further. For businesses, this might involve shutting down entire segments of the network. Once the threat is contained, IT teams can focus on identifying the ransomware strain, assessing the extent of the damage, and beginning the recovery process.

Clear communication during a ransomware incident is critical. Stakeholders, including employees, customers, and possibly law enforcement, should be informed of the situation and the steps being taken to resolve it. For businesses, transparency can help maintain customer trust and ensure that everyone involved understands the company's recovery efforts.

CHAPTER 5
Recovering from a Ransomware Attack

Even with the strongest defenses, no system is entirely immune to ransomware attacks. When ransomware strikes, it can leave a trail of encrypted files, locked systems, and disrupted operations. The road to recovery is often long and difficult, but with the right approach, it is possible to minimize damage, restore data, and regain control. In this chapter, we will explore the steps involved in recovering from a ransomware attack, covering both technical recovery and the broader implications of an attack on trust, operations, and long-term resilience.

IMMEDIATE RESPONSE: CONTAINING THE DAMAGE

The moment ransomware is detected, the first priority is to contain the damage and prevent further spread. Ransomware, especially sophisticated variants, can propagate quickly within networks, infecting multiple systems and corrupting backups. Immediate action is crucial to limit the scope of the attack.

The first step in containment is to disconnect the infected system or systems from the network. This prevents the ransomware from spreading to other devices and accessing shared resources. In organizations, this often involves shutting down affected segments of the network or temporarily disabling key services. Time is of the essence: the longer ransomware remains active in a network, the more damage it can cause.

Once the infected systems are isolated, it's important to avoid rebooting them or tampering with the encrypted files. In some cases, ransomware will delete encryption keys or escalate its destructive actions if it detects any tampering. For this reason, it is crucial to handle infected systems carefully until a proper plan for recovery is in place.

Assessing the Damage

After the immediate containment, the next step is assessing the damage caused by the ransomware attack. This assessment includes identifying which files and systems have been compromised, determining how the ransomware entered the system, and evaluating the overall impact on operations.

To start, security teams or forensic investigators should determine the specific type of ransomware involved. Many ransomware variants leave identifiable signatures, and some even provide hints within the ransom note about the ransomware family. Identifying the variant is essential because security researchers and cybersecurity firms may already have developed tools or solutions to decrypt certain types of ransomware.

Next, the extent of the damage must be evaluated. This involves determining which files have been encrypted, which systems have been affected, and whether any sensitive data has been exfiltrated. In the case of double extortion ransomware, attackers often steal data before encrypting it, so it is critical to assess whether any sensitive or personal information has been compromised.

Organizations should also consider the operational impact of the attack. For example, how much downtime has the attack caused? Which critical services have been disrupted? Understanding the full scope of the damage will help guide the recovery process and determine the necessary steps to restore normal operations.

Restoring from Backups

The most reliable way to recover from a ransomware attack without paying the ransom is by restoring systems from clean, uninfected backups. As discussed in previous chapters, having a solid backup strategy is essential to mitigating the impact of ransomware.

Once the affected systems have been isolated and the damage assessed, IT teams can begin the process of restoring data from backups. This involves wiping the infected systems clean and reinstalling the operating system and applications from scratch. Once the systems are restored to a clean state, the backup files can be reintroduced.

For individuals, restoring from backups might involve using external hard drives or cloud-based storage to recover personal documents, photos, and other files. For businesses, the process is more complex and may require restoring entire servers, databases, and network configurations. It is critical that the backups used in the restoration process were created before the ransomware infection occurred; otherwise, there is a risk of reinfection.

In addition to restoring data, businesses may need to restore critical services and applications to ensure that normal operations can resume. This could involve working with cloud providers, application vendors, or third-party services to bring everything back online.

Decryption Tools: When Paying the Ransom Isn't Necessary

In some cases, it is possible to recover data without resorting to backups or paying the ransom. Security researchers and cybersecurity firms have developed free decryption tools for certain ransomware strains. If the ransomware variant is well-known, victims may be able to use these tools to decrypt their files and regain access without paying.

Decryption tools are not available for all types of ransomware, and many modern strains use advanced encryption methods that are impossible to break. However, for older or less sophisticated ransomware, these tools can be a valuable resource. Organizations such as **No More Ransom**, a joint initiative by law enforcement agencies and private cybersecurity firms, provide a repository of free decryption tools for known ransomware variants.

Before attempting to use a decryption tool, it is important to ensure that it is legitimate and safe. Cybercriminals have been known to offer fake decryption tools that deliver even more malware to the victim's system. Always download decryption tools from trusted, verified sources to avoid further compromise.

The Dilemma of Paying the Ransom

When ransomware strikes, one of the most difficult decisions for victims is whether or not to pay the ransom. Cybersecurity experts universally advise against paying, as it funds criminal activities and encourages further attacks. Additionally, there is no guarantee that paying the ransom will lead to the recovery of data. Many victims who pay never receive the promised decryption key, or they find that their data has been permanently corrupted during the encryption process.

For businesses, the decision to pay the ransom can be even more complex. In some cases, paying the ransom may seem like the quickest way to recover critical operations and avoid prolonged downtime. However, this approach comes with significant risks. Even if the decryption key is provided, there may be hidden malware left behind, waiting to strike again.

Some companies have cyber insurance policies that cover ransomware payments, making the decision to pay more tempting. However, this raises ethical and practical concerns. Paying a ransom sets a dangerous precedent and may lead to more targeted attacks in the future. Additionally, paying the ransom does not absolve victims of potential legal liabilities, particularly if personal data has been compromised during the attack.

Ultimately, the decision to pay the ransom should be carefully weighed, and victims should explore all other recovery options before considering payment.

LEARNING FROM THE ATTACK: STRENGTHENING SECURITY POSTURE

Once the immediate crisis has been resolved and systems have been restored, it is essential to reflect on the attack and take steps to prevent future incidents. Ransomware attacks often reveal weaknesses in cybersecurity defenses, and these vulnerabilities must be addressed to avoid a repeat scenario.

Conducting a thorough post-mortem analysis is key to understanding how the ransomware breached the system and what can be done to prevent it from happening again. This analysis should cover the entry point of the ransomware, whether it was a phishing email, an unpatched vulnerability, or weak security practices. Once the root cause is identified, steps can be taken to close the security gap.

For businesses, this might involve implementing stronger security measures such as multifactor authentication (MFA), network segmentation, and regular security audits. It is also important to revisit the organization's backup strategy to ensure that backups are both frequent and secure. Furthermore, employee training should be updated to reflect the latest ransomware tactics, ensuring that staff remain vigilant.

Individuals, too, should review their security practices. This includes using stronger passwords, enabling MFA on personal accounts, and being cautious with email attachments and downloads. Installing and regularly updating antivirus software, as well as ensuring that system patches are applied promptly, can go a long way toward preventing future ransomware attacks.

Rebuilding Trust: Communicating with Stakeholders

Ransomware attacks can have a profound impact on trust, especially when personal data is involved. Whether it is a business dealing with customers, a government agency managing public services, or an individual communicating with personal contacts, transparency is key to rebuilding trust after an attack.

For businesses, it is crucial to communicate clearly and honestly with customers about the nature of the attack, what data may have been compromised, and what steps are being taken to prevent future incidents. Regulatory obligations may also require businesses to notify affected individuals and authorities, particularly if personal data has been breached.

Offering support, such as credit monitoring services or identity theft protection, can help ease concerns for customers whose data may have been exposed. Additionally, businesses should provide regular updates on their recovery efforts and security improvements to reassure stakeholders that they are taking the necessary steps to protect against future attacks.

CHAPTER 6
The Societal Impact of Ransomware

Ransomware is more than just a digital menace—it is a societal issue with wide-ranging consequences that ripple through industries, institutions, governments, and individuals. As ransomware attacks have escalated in both frequency and sophistication, their effects are being felt far beyond the victims directly targeted by these cybercriminals. From economic losses and public service disruptions to the erosion of trust in digital systems, ransomware is reshaping how societies think about cybersecurity, data protection, and digital infrastructure.

In this chapter, we will explore the broader implications of ransomware on society, delving into how these attacks affect critical sectors, public confidence, and even global politics. By understanding the far-reaching consequences of ransomware, we can better appreciate the urgency of addressing this growing threat.

Economic Fallout of Ransomware

Ransomware attacks are notoriously expensive, not only for the immediate victims but for the broader economy as well. The financial costs of a ransomware incident can be staggering, with some estimates suggesting that global losses from ransomware attacks exceed billions of dollars annually. These costs are not limited to ransom payments; they include the expenses associated with lost productivity, system downtime, data recovery, legal fees, regulatory fines, and reputational damage.

For businesses, the economic impact of ransomware can be catastrophic. Small and medium-sized enterprises (SMEs) are particularly vulnerable because they often lack the resources to recover quickly from an attack. For these organizations, even a short period of downtime can lead to significant financial strain, lost contracts, or permanent closure. Large enterprises, while better equipped to handle attacks, can still suffer losses in the millions of dollars when critical systems are taken offline.

Beyond direct financial losses, ransomware attacks also have broader economic implications. When major companies or institutions fall victim to ransomware, the effects can be felt across supply chains, affecting other businesses and consumers. For example, the 2021 attack on **Colonial Pipeline**, a critical fuel supplier in the United States, caused fuel shortages and price hikes across several states, demonstrating how ransomware can disrupt entire sectors and regions.

Disruption of Critical Infrastructure

Perhaps one of the most alarming trends in ransomware attacks is the targeting of critical infrastructure. Cybercriminals are increasingly setting their sights on sectors that provide essential services, such as healthcare, energy, transportation, and education. The motivation behind these attacks is simple: the more essential the service, the more likely the victim will pay the ransom to restore operations quickly.

The healthcare sector has become a prime target for ransomware attacks, especially during times of crisis like the COVID-19 pandemic. Hospitals, clinics, and healthcare providers rely on digital systems to manage patient records, coordinate care, and operate medical devices. A ransomware attack that disrupts these systems can put lives at risk. In fact, some hospitals have been forced to turn away patients or delay critical treatments during ransomware incidents, leading to devastating consequences.

Similarly, ransomware attacks on energy providers, transportation networks, and utilities pose a significant threat to public safety. As seen in the Colonial Pipeline attack, even a brief disruption to critical infrastructure can lead to widespread panic, supply chain issues, and economic fallout. These incidents underscore the growing importance of securing critical infrastructure against cyberattacks, as the consequences of failure could be dire.

THE PSYCHOLOGICAL AND SOCIAL IMPACT

Ransomware attacks also have profound psychological and social effects, especially when they target individuals or public institutions. The fear and uncertainty generated by ransomware can erode public confidence in digital systems, leading to widespread anxiety about the safety of personal information and the reliability of online services.

For individuals who fall victim to ransomware, the experience can be deeply unsettling. The sudden loss of access to personal files, photos, and important documents can feel like an invasion of privacy, leaving victims feeling vulnerable and violated. In some cases, victims are forced to weigh difficult decisions—such as paying a ransom or risking permanent loss of valuable data—which can create significant emotional distress.

The impact is even more pronounced when public institutions are targeted. Schools, government agencies, and healthcare providers are trusted to safeguard sensitive information and provide essential services. When these institutions are brought to a standstill by ransomware, public trust is shaken. Citizens may begin to question the ability of these organizations to protect their data and ensure continuity of services in the face of digital threats.

The social impact of ransomware is further compounded by the fact that many attacks go unreported. Some victims, particularly businesses, choose not to disclose ransomware incidents out of fear of reputational damage or legal repercussions. This lack of transparency can lead to underreporting of ransomware's true societal impact, making it difficult to fully understand the scope of the problem.

The Globalization of Ransomware Attacks

Ransomware is not confined to any one country or region; it is a global phenomenon. Cybercriminals operating in one part of the world can launch ransomware attacks on victims halfway across the globe, thanks to the borderless nature of the internet. This globalization of ransomware has introduced new challenges for law enforcement and policymakers, who must grapple with international jurisdictions, legal frameworks, and cooperation across borders.

Many ransomware groups operate from countries with limited or lax cybersecurity laws, making it difficult for international authorities to hold them accountable. Some of these groups are even suspected of having ties to nation-states, further complicating efforts to combat ransomware. In some cases, ransomware attacks have been linked to broader geopolitical conflicts, where state-sponsored hackers use ransomware as a tool of cyber warfare to destabilize critical infrastructure or exert political pressure on rival nations.

The global nature of ransomware also means that international cooperation is essential in the fight against cybercrime. Initiatives like the **No More Ransom** project, which brings together law enforcement agencies, cybersecurity firms, and governments, aim to provide global solutions to the ransomware problem. However, the sheer scale of the issue means that more coordinated efforts are needed to track down cybercriminals, dismantle their operations, and create a safer digital environment for everyone.

Ransomware and Cybersecurity Policy

The rise of ransomware has prompted significant changes in cybersecurity policy, both at the national and international levels. Governments and regulatory bodies are increasingly recognizing the threat posed by ransomware and are implementing new laws and regulations to address it.

In the wake of high-profile ransomware attacks, many countries have introduced stricter data protection regulations. For instance, the **European Union's General Data Protection Regulation (GDPR)** and similar laws around the world now hold organizations accountable for failing to protect personal data, with severe penalties for breaches. In some cases, failure to implement adequate cybersecurity measures can result in hefty fines, even if the breach is caused by a ransomware attack.

Governments are also investing in public-private partnerships to strengthen national cybersecurity defenses. Many critical sectors, such as energy, finance, and healthcare, are working closely with government agencies to share threat intelligence and develop coordinated responses to ransomware incidents. Cybersecurity awareness campaigns aimed at educating the public and businesses about the dangers of ransomware have also gained traction in recent years, with the goal of reducing the number of successful attacks.

At the international level, discussions around creating standardized cybersecurity protocols and improving cooperation between nations are ongoing. The need for a global framework to address ransomware is becoming more apparent, as cybercriminals continue to exploit legal loopholes and jurisdictional boundaries to evade capture.

The Ethics of Ransomware Payments

One of the most contentious issues surrounding ransomware is the ethics of paying ransoms. As discussed in previous chapters, paying a ransom can be tempting for victims who are desperate to recover their data and resume operations. However, this practice raises significant ethical and legal concerns.

Paying ransoms fuels the ransomware economy, incentivizing cybercriminals to continue their attacks. Every time a victim pays, it signals to the attackers that their methods are effective, encouraging them to target more victims. Additionally, there is no guarantee that paying the ransom will lead to the recovery of data. In some cases, cybercriminals take the money and disappear, leaving the victim without access to their files.

Governments and cybersecurity experts generally discourage ransom payments for these reasons. In fact, some countries have considered legislation that would ban businesses from paying ransoms altogether. The idea is that if fewer victims pay, ransomware attacks will become less profitable, leading to a decrease in their frequency. However, this approach is controversial, as it could leave victims, particularly in critical sectors like healthcare, with few options for recovery.

The debate over ransom payments also touches on broader questions about the role of insurance companies in ransomware incidents. Some cyber insurance policies cover ransomware payments, leading to concerns that insurance companies may be inadvertently supporting the ransomware business model. This has led to calls for tighter regulation of cyber insurance and greater scrutiny of how these policies are used in ransomware cases.

CHAPTER 7
The Future of Ransomware

As ransomware continues to evolve, it is clear that this form of cybercrime will remain a significant threat in the years to come. Cybercriminals are constantly adapting their tactics, seeking new ways to exploit vulnerabilities in both technology and human behavior. At the same time, advances in cybersecurity, legal frameworks, and global cooperation are working to counter this threat. In this chapter, we will explore the future of ransomware, examining emerging trends, potential developments in ransomware tactics, and the measures that governments, businesses, and individuals must take to stay ahead of cybercriminals.

THE EVOLUTION OF RANSOMWARE TACTICS

Ransomware has come a long way since its early days. Initially, ransomware attacks were relatively simple, targeting individual computers with basic encryption methods. Over time, however, ransomware has become increasingly sophisticated, with attackers employing advanced techniques to maximize damage and profit.

One of the most significant developments in recent years is the rise of **double extortion** ransomware. In these attacks, cybercriminals not only encrypt a victim's data but also steal it before locking the files. They then threaten to release sensitive information publicly if the ransom is not paid. This tactic adds an additional layer of pressure on victims, particularly businesses and organizations that are responsible for protecting confidential or sensitive data. Double extortion has proven to be highly effective in increasing the likelihood of ransom payments, and it is expected to continue evolving as ransomware groups look for new ways to apply pressure on their victims.

Another emerging tactic is the use of **ransomware-as-a-service (RaaS)**, where cybercriminals sell or lease their ransomware tools to other attackers. This model has made ransomware more accessible to a wider range of criminals, even those with limited technical skills. RaaS operators provide everything from the ransomware software itself to customer support, making it easy for aspiring attackers to launch their own campaigns. This trend has contributed to the rapid proliferation of ransomware attacks across the globe.

In the future, we can expect ransomware tactics to become even more targeted and personalized. Attackers are likely to use more sophisticated methods of social engineering, such as **deepfake** technology and **AI-driven phishing campaigns**, to trick victims into clicking malicious links or downloading infected files. As attackers refine their strategies, they will likely focus on high-value targets such as large corporations, government agencies, and critical infrastructure providers, where the potential for ransom payments is highest.

Ransomware and Emerging Technologies

As new technologies emerge, they will inevitably influence the evolution of ransomware. Some of these technologies will offer new opportunities for cybercriminals, while others will enhance the ability of defenders to protect against attacks. Understanding the relationship between ransomware and emerging technologies is crucial for anticipating future developments.

One of the most significant technological shifts on the horizon is the growing adoption of **5G networks**. While 5G promises faster internet speeds and enhanced connectivity, it also introduces new risks. The increased number of connected devices, from smartphones to Internet of Things (IoT) devices, creates a larger attack surface for cybercriminals to exploit. Ransomware attackers could potentially target IoT devices, such as smart home systems or industrial control systems, to disrupt operations and extort ransoms. The decentralized nature of 5G networks may also make it more difficult to detect and respond to attacks, as traditional network monitoring tools may struggle to keep up with the scale and complexity of 5G environments.

Another area of concern is the rise of **cryptocurrency**. While cryptocurrencies like Bitcoin have long been the preferred method of payment for ransomware attackers, the growing popularity of decentralized finance (DeFi) platforms and privacy-focused cryptocurrencies could make it even harder to trace ransom payments. These technologies allow cybercriminals to move money quickly and anonymously, complicating efforts to track down and prosecute ransomware groups. As ransomware payments increasingly flow through decentralized channels, law enforcement agencies will need to develop new strategies for disrupting these financial networks.

At the same time, advancements in **artificial intelligence (AI)** and **machine learning (ML)** hold promise for improving ransomware defenses. AI-driven security tools can analyze vast amounts of data in real-time, identifying patterns and anomalies that could indicate a ransomware attack. These tools can also automate responses, such as isolating infected systems or blocking malicious traffic, reducing the time it takes to contain an attack. As AI continues to improve, it will become a valuable asset in the fight against ransomware, helping organizations stay one step ahead of cybercriminals.

However, it is important to note that cybercriminals are also likely to leverage AI for their own purposes. AI can be used to develop more sophisticated malware, automate the process of scanning for vulnerabilities, and even create more convincing phishing emails. As both attackers and defenders incorporate AI into their arsenals, the future of ransomware will be shaped by an ongoing arms race between these two sides.

The Role of Governments and Regulation

Governments around the world are recognizing that ransomware is not just a private-sector problem but a national security threat. As ransomware attacks increasingly target critical infrastructure, public services, and large corporations, governments are stepping up their efforts to combat this growing menace.

One key area where governments are focusing their efforts is in **legislation and regulation**. Many countries are introducing new laws aimed at improving cybersecurity standards and holding organizations accountable for protecting their data. For example, the **European Union's General Data Protection Regulation (GDPR)** imposes strict penalties on organizations that fail to safeguard personal data, including in the event of ransomware attacks. Similarly, the **U.S. Cybersecurity and Infrastructure Security Agency (CISA)** has been working to implement new guidelines and frameworks to strengthen national cybersecurity.

In addition to regulatory measures, governments are increasingly investing in **public-private partnerships** to address the ransomware threat. These partnerships facilitate the sharing of threat intelligence between government agencies and the private sector, allowing for more coordinated responses to ransomware incidents.

Governments are also encouraging businesses to adopt stronger cybersecurity practices, such as regular vulnerability assessments, multifactor authentication, and employee training programs.

International cooperation is another critical aspect of the fight against ransomware. Cybercriminals often operate across borders, making it difficult for any single country to take effective action. As a result, governments are working together to develop global strategies for combating ransomware. Initiatives like **INTERPOL's cybercrime program** and the **No More Ransom** project, which provides free decryption tools to ransomware victims, are examples of the collaborative efforts needed to address this global issue.

Looking ahead, we can expect to see more governments enacting **ransomware-specific legislation**, such as laws that prohibit paying ransoms or require mandatory reporting of ransomware incidents. While these measures are intended to reduce the profitability of ransomware attacks, they may also raise new challenges for businesses, particularly those facing critical operational disruptions due to an attack.

The Future of Ransomware Defense

As ransomware attacks become more advanced, organizations must adopt a more proactive and holistic approach to cybersecurity. The future of ransomware defense will be shaped by several key trends, including the increased use of **zero-trust architectures**, **cloud-based security solutions**, and **behavioral analytics**.

Zero-trust architectures represent a fundamental shift in how organizations approach cybersecurity. Rather than assuming that everything within a network is trustworthy, zero-trust models require constant verification of users, devices, and applications, regardless of their location within the network. This approach minimizes the risk of ransomware spreading unchecked within a network, as every access request is subject to rigorous scrutiny. As ransomware tactics become more sophisticated, zero-trust architectures will likely become a cornerstone of cybersecurity strategies.

The growing reliance on cloud services also presents new challenges and opportunities for ransomware defense. On one hand, cloud environments are vulnerable to ransomware attacks, particularly if access controls and security measures are not properly configured. On the other hand, cloud providers offer advanced security features, such as **automated backups**, **real-time monitoring**, and **encryption**, which can help organizations detect and respond to ransomware more effectively. As more businesses migrate to the cloud, securing cloud environments will become a critical aspect of ransomware defense.

Finally, the future of ransomware defense will increasingly rely on **behavioral analytics**. This technology uses machine learning algorithms to analyze user behavior and detect anomalies that could indicate a ransomware attack. For example, if a user suddenly starts accessing a large number of files at once, behavioral analytics tools can flag this activity as suspicious and trigger an automatic response. By focusing on user behavior rather than static signatures, these tools can identify and stop ransomware attacks before they cause significant damage.

The Human Element: Education and Awareness

While technological solutions play a crucial role in defending against ransomware, the human element remains one of the most important factors in preventing attacks. Ransomware often relies on social engineering tactics to trick users into clicking malicious links, downloading infected files, or revealing sensitive information. As a result, **education and awareness** will continue to be a critical component of ransomware defense in the future.

Organizations must invest in regular **cybersecurity training** for employees, teaching them how to recognize phishing emails, avoid suspicious downloads, and report potential threats. Cybersecurity awareness programs should be dynamic and adaptive, reflecting the latest trends in ransomware tactics. For example, as attackers begin to use more advanced techniques like deepfakes or AI-generated emails, employees must be equipped with the knowledge to identify these threats.

For individuals, staying informed about cybersecurity best practices is equally important. Simple steps like enabling **multifactor authentication**, using **strong passwords**, and being cautious with email attachments can go a long way toward preventing ransomware infections. As ransomware continues to evolve, a culture of cybersecurity awareness will be essential to protecting both individuals and organizations from future attacks.

CHAPTER 8
The Role of Cyber Insurance in Ransomware Defense

As ransomware has become one of the most pervasive forms of cybercrime, a growing number of organizations and individuals have turned to **cyber insurance** as part of their defense strategy. Cyber insurance, which provides financial protection against the damages caused by cyberattacks, has quickly become an essential tool for managing the risks posed by ransomware. However, the relationship between ransomware and cyber insurance is complex and, in some cases, controversial.

In this chapter, we will explore the role of cyber insurance in ransomware defense, examining how it works, its benefits, its drawbacks, and the ethical dilemmas it raises. We will also look at how the cyber insurance industry is evolving in response to the rising threat of ransomware and what this means for the future of cybersecurity.

How Cyber Insurance Works

At its core, cyber insurance is designed to protect businesses and individuals from the financial fallout of a cyberattack. Just as traditional insurance policies cover damages from accidents, fires, or theft, cyber insurance policies provide coverage for various costs associated with cyber incidents. These costs can include data recovery, legal fees, notification costs (such as informing customers of a data breach), and, in some cases, the ransom payment itself.

For businesses, cyber insurance policies are tailored to meet specific needs, depending on the nature and size of the organization. For example, a small business might take out a policy that covers ransomware-related costs up to a certain limit, while a large corporation with more extensive digital infrastructure might require a higher level of coverage. Cyber insurance also often includes access to experts who can assist with incident response, helping businesses mitigate the damage caused by an attack.

The scope of coverage typically depends on the specifics of the policy. Some policies cover the ransom payment directly, while others focus on compensating for lost revenue due to downtime or business interruptions caused by a ransomware attack. Additionally, many policies cover the costs of forensics investigations to determine how the attack occurred and what data was compromised.

The Benefits of Cyber Insurance

One of the primary benefits of cyber insurance is that it provides businesses with a financial safety net in the event of a ransomware attack. For organizations that fall victim to an attack, the costs can be staggering—ranging from ransom payments to the expenses of restoring compromised systems and reputational damage. Without cyber insurance, many businesses, particularly small and medium-sized enterprises (SMEs), may not have the resources to recover fully.

Cyber insurance also plays a critical role in reducing downtime. Ransomware attacks can bring businesses to a complete standstill, preventing them from accessing their systems and data. For companies that rely heavily on digital infrastructure, this can lead to significant losses in productivity and revenue. Cyber insurance helps mitigate these losses by providing the necessary funds to restore systems as quickly as possible, allowing businesses to resume normal operations.

Moreover, cyber insurance policies often come with access to specialized cybersecurity services, such as incident response teams, forensic investigators, and legal counsel. These services are invaluable during the immediate aftermath of a ransomware attack, helping businesses manage the crisis, contain the damage, and navigate the legal and regulatory landscape.

Finally, cyber insurance provides peace of mind. In today's digital world, the risk of a ransomware attack is ever-present. Knowing that they have insurance coverage can help organizations focus on their core operations without constantly worrying about the financial implications of a potential attack.

The Drawbacks and Ethical Concerns

While cyber insurance offers many benefits, it also has its share of drawbacks and ethical challenges, particularly when it comes to ransomware. One of the most significant concerns is that cyber insurance may inadvertently fuel the ransomware economy by encouraging victims to pay the ransom.

Many cyber insurance policies cover the cost of paying ransoms, which can create a moral hazard. Cybercriminals are well aware that insurance companies are often willing to pay ransoms quickly to resolve the situation, leading them to target insured organizations more frequently. In some cases, ransomware groups have even adjusted their ransom demands based on their knowledge of the victim's insurance coverage, increasing the amounts they demand from well-insured companies.

This practice raises a broader ethical dilemma: by paying ransoms, insurance companies (and by extension, their clients) may be perpetuating the cycle of ransomware attacks. Every time a ransom is paid, it reinforces the notion that ransomware is a profitable venture, encouraging more attacks. For this reason, many cybersecurity experts and government agencies discourage paying ransoms, arguing that doing so only emboldens cybercriminals.

Another concern is that some businesses may become overly reliant on their insurance coverage and neglect to invest in robust cybersecurity measures. If a company knows that it is insured against ransomware, it may be less motivated to implement preventative measures such as employee training, regular backups, or network segmentation. This complacency can make organizations more vulnerable to attacks, ultimately driving up the costs of ransomware incidents.

The Evolution of the Cyber Insurance Industry

As ransomware attacks have grown in frequency and severity, the cyber insurance industry has been forced to adapt. Insurers are now facing increasing pressure to manage the risks associated with ransomware, which has led to changes in how policies are structured, priced, and underwritten.

In recent years, the cost of cyber insurance premiums has risen sharply due to the sheer number of ransomware claims. Insurers are finding it increasingly difficult to absorb the costs of these attacks, particularly when large payouts are required to cover ransom payments or the extensive recovery efforts following an attack. As a result, many insurers are raising premiums or limiting the coverage they provide for ransomware-related incidents.

Some insurers are also placing stricter requirements on policyholders to ensure that they are taking proactive steps to prevent ransomware attacks. For example, businesses seeking cyber insurance may now be required to demonstrate that they have implemented basic cybersecurity measures, such as multi-factor authentication, regular patching, and employee training programs. These requirements help reduce the likelihood of a successful attack and, in turn, lower the potential costs for insurers.

Additionally, some insurance companies are beginning to exclude ransom payments from their policies altogether or offer policies with lower limits on ransom coverage. This shift reflects a growing recognition that paying ransoms is not a sustainable long-term solution to the ransomware problem. Instead, insurers are focusing on offering coverage for other costs associated with ransomware, such as data recovery, legal fees, and business interruption losses.

THE FUTURE OF CYBER INSURANCE AND RANSOMWARE

As the ransomware landscape continues to evolve, so too will the role of cyber insurance. One key area of focus for the future is the development of **cyber risk assessments** that help insurers and businesses better understand their vulnerabilities and manage their risks. By conducting thorough assessments of their digital infrastructure, businesses can identify weak points that could be exploited by ransomware attackers and take steps to address them before an attack occurs.

Cyber insurers are also likely to invest more heavily in **predictive analytics** and **machine learning** to improve their ability to assess risk and predict the likelihood of a ransomware attack. By analyzing vast amounts of data on past attacks, insurers can develop models that help identify which industries, organizations, or regions are most at risk of being targeted. This information can then be used to tailor policies and premiums more accurately.

Another potential development is the creation of **cyber insurance consortiums**, where multiple insurers pool their resources to cover large-scale ransomware incidents. These consortiums could help distribute the financial risk of ransomware attacks across a broader base, making it easier for insurers to offer affordable coverage while still protecting businesses from catastrophic losses.

At the same time, the cyber insurance industry will need to grapple with the ethical questions surrounding ransom payments. Some industry experts have suggested that governments may eventually impose regulations on the payment of ransoms, either banning them outright or requiring businesses to seek approval before making a payment. If such regulations are implemented, the role of cyber insurance in ransomware defense could change dramatically, with insurers focusing more on helping businesses recover without paying ransoms.

CHAPTER 9
Real-World Ransomware Case Studies

To understand the true impact of ransomware, we must examine real-world incidents where this form of cyberattack has disrupted businesses, healthcare systems, government agencies, and individual lives. These case studies illustrate the devastating effects of ransomware and the varied responses to such attacks, providing valuable lessons for both organizations and cybersecurity professionals. In this chapter, we will explore several high-profile ransomware attacks, analyzing how they unfolded, the steps taken to resolve them, and the broader implications for ransomware defense.

CASE STUDY 1: THE WANNACRY ATTACK (2017)

The **WannaCry ransomware attack** in May 2017 is one of the most infamous ransomware incidents in history. Targeting computers running Microsoft Windows, WannaCry spread rapidly across the globe, infecting over 230,000 computers in more than 150 countries within a matter of days. The ransomware exploited a vulnerability in Windows' Server Message Block (SMB) protocol, which had been previously identified and patched by Microsoft. However, many organizations had not yet applied the patch, leaving their systems vulnerable to the attack.

Once installed, WannaCry encrypted files on the infected computers and displayed a ransom demand for payment in Bitcoin. Victims were warned that if they did not pay the ransom within a few days, the ransom amount would increase, and after a certain period, the encrypted files would be permanently deleted.

The impact of WannaCry was particularly severe in the healthcare sector. The **UK's National Health Service (NHS)** was one of the hardest-hit organizations, with thousands of appointments and surgeries canceled, and patients turned away from hospitals due to the disruption of critical IT systems. Medical devices, such as MRI scanners, were rendered inoperable, and doctors were unable to access patient records. The global shipping giant **Maersk** was also severely affected, losing hundreds of millions of dollars in revenue as its logistics and port operations ground to a halt.

WannaCry's rapid spread was ultimately halted by a cybersecurity researcher who discovered a “kill switch” in the code, which prevented the ransomware from continuing to propagate. Despite this, the damage had already been done, and WannaCry highlighted the devastating potential of ransomware to disrupt essential services.

The WannaCry attack underscored several critical lessons:

- **Patch management is essential**: The vulnerability exploited by WannaCry had been patched by Microsoft two months prior to the attack, but many organizations failed to apply the update in time. This emphasizes the importance of keeping software up to date to prevent known vulnerabilities from being exploited.
- **Legacy systems are high-risk targets**: Many of the systems affected by WannaCry were running outdated versions of Windows, which were no longer supported by Microsoft. Legacy systems that are not regularly updated or maintained are particularly vulnerable to ransomware attacks.
- **Ransomware can have life-threatening consequences**: The disruption of healthcare services during the WannaCry attack highlighted how ransomware can endanger human lives, not just disrupt businesses.

Case Study 2: The Colonial Pipeline Attack (2021)

In May 2021, a ransomware attack on **Colonial Pipeline**, one of the largest fuel pipelines in the United States, caused widespread panic and fuel shortages along the East Coast. The attack, attributed to the ransomware group **DarkSide**, resulted in the temporary shutdown of the pipeline, which supplies nearly half of the fuel used on the East Coast.

The attackers gained access to Colonial Pipeline's systems by exploiting a compromised password that had been used for a remote access VPN account. Once inside, the ransomware encrypted key files, and the attackers demanded a ransom of nearly $5 million in Bitcoin. Faced with the potential for prolonged disruption to fuel supplies, Colonial Pipeline chose to pay the ransom, though it still took several days to fully restore operations.

The attack on Colonial Pipeline had significant ripple effects beyond the company itself. The pipeline's shutdown led to fuel shortages and price spikes in several states, with long lines forming at gas stations as consumers rushed to stock up on fuel. The incident also raised concerns about the vulnerability of critical infrastructure to cyberattacks and prompted the U.S. government to take action. President Joe

Biden signed an executive order to improve the nation's cybersecurity, calling for stronger standards for critical infrastructure and increased collaboration between the public and private sectors.

Key takeaways from the Colonial Pipeline attack include:

- **Critical infrastructure is a prime target**: Ransomware attackers are increasingly targeting critical infrastructure, such as energy, transportation, and healthcare systems, where disruption can cause widespread harm and increase the likelihood of ransom payments.
- **Multi-factor authentication is crucial**: The attackers gained access to Colonial Pipeline's systems through a compromised password. Implementing multi-factor authentication (MFA) could have prevented the attack by adding an extra layer of security to remote access systems.
- **Government intervention is necessary**: The Colonial Pipeline attack highlighted the need for stronger government oversight and regulation of cybersecurity in critical infrastructure sectors. It also demonstrated the importance of public-private partnerships in responding to and preventing ransomware attacks.

Case Study 3: The Kaseya VSA Supply Chain Attack (2021)

In July 2021, the ransomware group **REvil** launched a sophisticated supply chain attack on **Kaseya**, a company that provides IT management and remote monitoring software to managed service providers (MSPs). The attackers exploited a vulnerability in Kaseya's **Virtual System Administrator (VSA)** software, using it to push ransomware to hundreds of businesses around the world through their MSPs.

The attack affected thousands of organizations, from small businesses to large corporations, as MSPs were used as conduits to spread the ransomware. REvil demanded a ransom of $70 million in Bitcoin for a universal decryption key, though individual companies were also targeted with separate ransom demands. The attack had a particularly devastating impact on **Coop**, a major Swedish supermarket chain, which was forced to close nearly all of its 800 stores for several days because its cash register systems were rendered inoperable by the ransomware.

Kaseya responded quickly by shutting down its VSA servers and working with law enforcement and cybersecurity firms to contain the attack. The U.S. government also became involved, as the attack was seen as a significant threat to the global supply chain. Ultimately, a decryption key was obtained, though the exact circumstances of how it was acquired remain unclear.

The Kaseya attack illustrated several important lessons:

- **Supply chain attacks amplify the impact of ransomware**: By targeting a software provider that serves multiple businesses, ransomware attackers can significantly increase the scale of their attacks. Supply chain vulnerabilities are a growing concern in the cybersecurity landscape.
- **Prompt response is critical**: Kaseya's quick decision to shut down its VSA servers helped limit the spread of the ransomware and prevented further damage. Organizations need to have well-prepared incident response plans to act swiftly in the event of an attack.
- **Third-party security is essential**: Businesses that rely on third-party software providers must ensure that those providers adhere to strong security practices. The security of the supply chain is only as strong as its weakest link.

Case Study 4: The Ryuk Ransomware on Hospitals (2018-2020)

Between 2018 and 2020, hospitals across the United States were repeatedly targeted by the **Ryuk ransomware**, which caused significant disruptions to healthcare services and posed serious risks to patient care. Ryuk, a ransomware variant associated with the **Wizard Spider** cybercriminal group, is known for targeting large organizations and demanding high ransoms, often in the millions of dollars.

The Ryuk attacks on hospitals were particularly damaging because they occurred at a time when many healthcare providers were already struggling with the demands of the COVID-19 pandemic. Hospitals found themselves unable to access patient records, schedule appointments, or manage critical medical equipment. In some cases, hospitals were forced to divert patients to other facilities, potentially delaying lifesaving treatments.

Despite the serious consequences of these attacks, many hospitals opted to pay the ransoms in order to restore their systems quickly. However, paying the ransom did not always guarantee a smooth recovery, as some hospitals experienced prolonged downtime or incomplete decryption of their data.

The Ryuk attacks highlighted several key issues:

- **Healthcare systems are prime targets for ransomware**: Hospitals and healthcare providers are particularly vulnerable to ransomware because of their reliance on digital systems and the urgency of patient care. Cybercriminals exploit this urgency, knowing that hospitals are more likely to pay ransoms to restore operations.
- **Cybersecurity in healthcare is critical**: The attacks demonstrated the need for hospitals to invest in stronger cybersecurity measures, such as regular backups, network segmentation, and employee training. The protection of patient data and the continuity of care must be top priorities for healthcare providers.
- **Paying the ransom is not a guarantee**: Even when hospitals paid the ransom, some did not receive a fully functional decryption key, and others experienced additional downtime during the recovery process. This underscores the risks of relying on ransom payments as a solution to ransomware attacks.

CHAPTER 10
Legal and Regulatory Landscape of Ransomware

The global rise of ransomware attacks has not only raised alarms within the business and technology sectors but has also caught the attention of governments and international law enforcement agencies. Ransomware, which transcends national borders, presents significant legal and regulatory challenges. Addressing these challenges requires coordination across multiple jurisdictions, as cybercriminals often operate from countries with lax enforcement or where prosecution is difficult.

In this chapter, we will explore the evolving legal and regulatory frameworks designed to combat ransomware. We will examine the difficulties in prosecuting ransomware attacks, the role of government regulations, international cooperation efforts, and the ethical dilemmas surrounding ransom payments. Finally, we will discuss the potential future direction of ransomware laws and policies.

CHALLENGES OF PROSECUTING RANSOMWARE ATTACKS

One of the biggest hurdles in dealing with ransomware from a legal perspective is the challenge of prosecution. Cybercriminals who deploy ransomware often operate anonymously and from foreign countries, making it difficult for law enforcement to track them down and bring them to justice.

Cybercriminals use sophisticated techniques to hide their identities and locations, including the use of **Tor networks**, **VPNs**, and **cryptocurrencies** like Bitcoin, which provide a high degree of anonymity. This makes it incredibly hard for investigators to trace the ransom payments back to the perpetrators. Even when the identities of the attackers are known, they may be based in countries that do not have extradition agreements or cooperative relationships with the countries where the victims are located, further complicating efforts to arrest and prosecute them.

For example, many ransomware groups operate out of regions with limited law enforcement cooperation, such as Russia, Eastern Europe, and certain parts of Asia. These regions provide a relative safe haven for cybercriminals, as local authorities may be either unwilling or unable to take action against them. This global nature of ransomware attacks means that addressing them requires cooperation across borders, involving multiple countries, agencies, and legal systems.

Government Regulations and Ransomware Policy

In response to the growing threat of ransomware, governments around the world have begun implementing regulations and policies aimed at strengthening cybersecurity practices and holding organizations accountable for data breaches.

In the United States, several key regulatory frameworks have been put in place to address the risks posed by ransomware and other forms of cyberattacks. These include:

- **The Cybersecurity Information Sharing Act (CISA),** which encourages the sharing of cyber threat information between the private sector and the federal government. This act aims to improve the collective ability to detect, prevent, and respond to cyberattacks by promoting collaboration between public and private entities.
- **The General Data Protection Regulation (GDPR)** in the European Union has also had a significant impact on

ransomware response. GDPR mandates that companies must report data breaches to regulatory authorities within 72 hours of discovery. Failure to comply with this requirement can result in hefty fines. This regulation has prompted organizations to strengthen their cybersecurity measures and implement more robust incident response plans to ensure they can quickly detect and report breaches, including those caused by ransomware.

Additionally, the Biden administration in the United States has taken a more aggressive stance on ransomware, particularly in the wake of the **Colonial Pipeline attack**. In 2021, the administration issued an **Executive Order on Improving the Nation's Cybersecurity**, which called for stronger security standards for federal agencies and critical infrastructure sectors. The order also mandated increased collaboration between the public and private sectors, particularly regarding the sharing of cyber threat intelligence.

One of the most notable developments in ransomware policy is the increased scrutiny on ransom payments. Governments, particularly in the U.S., have begun discouraging or outright prohibiting the payment of ransoms in some cases. For instance, the U.S. Department of the Treasury's **Office of Foreign Assets Control (OFAC)** issued advisories warning that companies who pay ransoms to sanctioned entities or individuals could face legal penalties. This has raised questions about the legality of paying ransoms and the potential consequences for businesses that do so.

International Cooperation and the Fight Against Ransomware

Given the international nature of ransomware, effective enforcement and regulation require collaboration among countries. While ransomware attacks are global in scope, responses to them are often fragmented due to differences in national laws, enforcement capabilities, and priorities.

One example of international cooperation is **Europol's Joint Cybercrime Action Taskforce (J-CAT)**, which brings together cybercrime experts from across Europe and partner countries to investigate and combat large-scale cybercriminal activities, including ransomware. J-CAT has been instrumental in coordinating international efforts to disrupt ransomware groups, share intelligence, and prosecute cybercriminals.

Another major initiative is the **No More Ransom** project, launched in 2016 by Europol, the Dutch National Police, and cybersecurity firms. The project provides free decryption tools for victims of ransomware and aims to educate the public about ransomware prevention. Through collaboration with law enforcement and cybersecurity companies around the world, No More Ransom has helped tens of thousands of victims recover their data without paying the ransom.

In the U.S., the **FBI** plays a central role in coordinating the response to ransomware attacks. The FBI collaborates with international partners, including **INTERPOL**, to track down ransomware operators and recover ransom payments. However, despite these efforts, the global nature of ransomware remains a significant obstacle to effective enforcement.

The Ethical Dilemmas of Ransom Payments

The question of whether to pay a ransom is one of the most contentious issues surrounding ransomware attacks. On one hand, businesses that fall victim to ransomware are often faced with a stark choice: pay the ransom and hope to regain access to their systems or refuse to pay and risk losing valuable data and incurring prolonged downtime.

Paying the ransom may seem like the easiest solution, especially for organizations that rely on quick recovery to maintain operations. However, paying the ransom presents several ethical and practical concerns. First and foremost, paying a ransom does not guarantee that the attackers will honor their word and provide a functioning decryption key. There have been numerous instances where victims paid the ransom but were left unable to recover their data, or where additional ransom demands were made after the initial payment.

Furthermore, by paying the ransom, victims are effectively funding criminal organizations. This creates a vicious cycle, as each successful ransom payment emboldens ransomware groups to continue their attacks, knowing that victims are likely to pay. It also incentivizes the development of more sophisticated ransomware strains and attack techniques.

Governments, including the U.S., have taken a firm stance against paying ransoms, arguing that doing so only encourages further attacks. However, the decision to pay or not to pay remains a difficult one, particularly for organizations that face severe financial or operational consequences as a result of the attack.

The Future of Ransomware Laws and Policies

As ransomware continues to evolve, so too will the legal and regulatory frameworks designed to combat it. In the coming years, we can expect to see several key trends in ransomware regulation:

- **Stricter Regulations on Critical Infrastructure**: Governments will likely introduce more stringent cybersecurity requirements for critical infrastructure sectors, such as healthcare, energy, and finance. These regulations may include mandatory security audits, incident reporting requirements, and penalties for failing to implement adequate security measures.
- **Increased Focus on Supply Chain Security**: Ransomware attacks that target supply chains, such as the **Kaseya VSA** attack, have highlighted the need for stronger security across third-party vendors and service providers. Future regulations may require businesses to assess the cybersecurity practices of their suppliers and ensure that they meet certain standards.

- **Crackdown on Cryptocurrencies**: As ransomware attackers continue to demand payment in cryptocurrencies, governments are likely to intensify their efforts to regulate and monitor cryptocurrency transactions. This could include stricter **Know Your Customer (KYC)** requirements for cryptocurrency exchanges and greater collaboration between regulators and law enforcement agencies to track and freeze illicit funds.
- **Global Cooperation**: The fight against ransomware will increasingly require coordinated international efforts. Governments may work together to establish global norms for ransomware response, such as guidelines on ransom payments, information sharing, and joint law enforcement actions.

CHAPTER 11
The Psychological Impact of Ransomware

Ransomware attacks are often discussed in terms of their financial costs and operational disruptions, but their impact extends far beyond these tangible losses. The psychological toll that ransomware exacts on individuals and organizations is profound, affecting victims in ways that are often overlooked. Whether it is a business facing potential closure due to an attack or an individual whose personal files are held hostage, the emotional strain can be severe.

In this chapter, we will delve into the psychological effects of ransomware on victims. We will explore the immediate emotional responses to an attack, the long-term psychological effects, and the impact of such attacks on trust and confidence in technology. Finally, we will discuss strategies that can help victims cope with the mental and emotional strain of ransomware incidents.

Immediate Emotional Reactions to a Ransomware Attack

The discovery of a ransomware attack typically triggers a wide range of intense emotions. Victims often experience feelings of shock, fear, and helplessness upon realizing that their valuable files or systems have been locked, and they are being extorted for money to regain access. The realization that they are at the mercy of cybercriminals can induce a strong sense of vulnerability.

Shock is one of the most common immediate reactions. The sudden and unexpected nature of ransomware attacks catches victims off guard. For businesses, this can result in chaos as employees scramble to understand the scope of the attack, assess the damage, and begin the process of recovery. For individuals, the shock may be accompanied by a sense of disbelief, especially if the ransomware targets deeply personal files such as family photos, important documents, or financial records.

Fear and anxiety quickly follow the initial shock. Victims often fear that they will lose their data forever if they do not comply with the ransom demand. For businesses, there is the additional fear of reputational damage, loss of clients, or even lawsuits from affected stakeholders. Individuals may worry about the loss of sensitive personal information and the potential for identity theft or further exploitation.

In both cases, victims feel a sense of **helplessness**. Ransomware attacks effectively strip away control, leaving victims uncertain about how to proceed. The attackers hold all the power, and victims may feel paralyzed as they weigh their options, unsure whether paying the ransom will actually lead to data recovery.

The Long-Term Psychological Impact

While the immediate emotional responses to ransomware can be intense, the long-term psychological effects are equally concerning. For many victims, the trauma of a ransomware attack lingers long after the event itself. These effects can manifest in several ways, including:

1. **Chronic Stress**: Ransomware attacks often result in a protracted recovery process, especially for businesses that need to restore systems, rebuild trust, and mitigate financial losses. The ongoing stress of dealing with the aftermath of an attack, coupled with the uncertainty of future threats, can take a significant toll on victims' mental health. For individuals, stress may stem from the loss of irreplaceable personal files or the financial burden of trying to recover from the attack.
2. **Anxiety and Paranoia**: Victims of ransomware may develop heightened anxiety or paranoia about their digital security. They may become overly cautious about

using the internet, downloading files, or opening emails, fearing that they could fall victim to another attack. This constant fear of being targeted again can disrupt both personal and professional lives, leading to a diminished sense of safety online.

3. **Loss of Trust in Technology**: Ransomware attacks can shatter victims' confidence in the digital tools and systems they rely on. For businesses, the attack may expose weaknesses in their cybersecurity infrastructure, eroding trust in their IT departments or third-party vendors. For individuals, the loss of personal data may lead to a deep skepticism about the safety of storing important information digitally. This loss of trust can make victims reluctant to adopt new technologies or participate in digital transactions, limiting their engagement with the digital world.

4. **Depression and Guilt**: Some victims of ransomware, particularly business leaders or IT professionals, may experience feelings of guilt or failure, believing that they should have done more to prevent the attack. This guilt can contribute to depression, especially if the attack results in significant financial losses, job losses, or the closure of a business. In cases where individuals lose irreplaceable personal files, they may experience grief akin to mourning a loss, leading to prolonged feelings of sadness or despair.

THE RIPPLE EFFECT: IMPACT ON ORGANIZATIONAL CULTURE

In the case of businesses, ransomware attacks do not just affect individuals—they can have a profound impact on organizational culture. Employees may feel demoralized or insecure following an attack, particularly if they were responsible for cybersecurity or played a role in the organization's response to the incident.

The fear of another attack can lead to a culture of **hyper-vigilance**, where employees become overly cautious about their actions online, potentially stifling creativity and productivity. At the same time, a **blame culture** may emerge, with employees pointing fingers at one another or at leadership for perceived failures in preventing the attack. This can create a toxic work environment, undermining collaboration and trust within the organization.

For IT teams, ransomware incidents often result in **burnout**. The pressure to restore systems quickly, combined with the responsibility of preventing future attacks, can lead to overwork and emotional exhaustion. Cybersecurity professionals, in particular, may feel the weight of the attack acutely, as they are often blamed for not having anticipated or stopped it. This can lead to high turnover rates, as employees seek to escape the stress and stigma of being associated with the attack.

COPING WITH THE EMOTIONAL AND PSYCHOLOGICAL AFTERMATH

Given the significant psychological toll of ransomware, it is essential for victims—whether individuals or organizations—to have strategies in place to cope with the emotional and mental effects. A key part of this process is recognizing that ransomware is not just a technical issue; it also requires emotional resilience and psychological support.

1. **Acceptance and Perspective**: For many victims, accepting that ransomware is an external threat beyond their control is the first step toward recovery. While it is natural to feel guilt or frustration, it is important to understand that cybercriminals specifically target vulnerabilities, and no one is immune. Gaining perspective on the situation can help alleviate feelings of personal failure or guilt.
2. **Emotional Support**: For businesses, providing emotional support to employees affected by the attack is crucial. This may involve offering counseling services, creating open lines of communication to address concerns, and promoting a culture of collective recovery rather than blame. Similarly, individuals who

have been targeted by ransomware should not hesitate to seek support from friends, family, or mental health professionals to cope with the emotional aftermath.

3. **Education and Empowerment**: Knowledge is a powerful antidote to fear. Educating both employees and individuals about ransomware, cybersecurity best practices, and preventive measures can help restore a sense of control and empowerment. Understanding how ransomware works, how to avoid it, and what steps to take if it happens again can alleviate anxiety and foster confidence in the future.
4. **Resilience and Preparedness**: The psychological impact of ransomware can be mitigated by focusing on resilience and preparedness. For businesses, this means investing in strong cybersecurity practices, conducting regular backups, and developing a robust incident response plan. For individuals, practicing good cyber hygiene—such as using multi-factor authentication and regularly updating software—can reduce the risk of falling victim to ransomware. Being prepared for future threats can help victims regain a sense of control and reduce the emotional toll of future attacks.

CHAPTER 12
Global Efforts in Combating Ransomware

As ransomware continues to evolve and expand, the fight against this growing cyber threat has become a global effort. Governments, cybersecurity organizations, and international bodies are joining forces to curb the rise of ransomware attacks, employing a mix of legislation, technological innovation, and collaborative initiatives.

In this chapter, we will explore how different countries and international organizations are addressing the ransomware crisis. We will examine the role of international cooperation in fighting cybercrime, the development of new regulations, and the future of law enforcement in the digital space. Additionally, we will discuss the increasing pressure on businesses and organizations to comply with cybersecurity standards as part of these global efforts.

Governmental Action Against Ransomware

Countries around the world are increasingly recognizing ransomware as a serious national security threat. Governments are taking steps to combat ransomware through a combination of legal reforms, sanctions, and investment in cybersecurity infrastructure. For example, in the United States, ransomware has been classified as a national security priority, leading to a more aggressive approach to tracking and dismantling ransomware groups.

Sanctions on ransomware groups and their facilitators have become a common strategy. By targeting the financial infrastructure of ransomware operators—particularly those based in countries with lenient cybercrime regulations—governments aim to disrupt the flow of illicit gains. These sanctions also extend to cryptocurrency exchanges that fail to implement anti-money laundering measures, as such platforms are often used to launder ransom payments.

Other countries, such as **the European Union**, have adopted a regulatory approach. The EU's **General Data Protection Regulation (GDPR)** imposes strict rules on data protection and breach notification, compelling organizations to strengthen their defenses against ransomware attacks. Similar laws in other regions, such as **China's Cybersecurity Law** and **India's Personal Data**

Protection Bill, are putting pressure on companies to prioritize cybersecurity.

Governments are also investing in public awareness campaigns and cybersecurity training programs to equip citizens and businesses with the knowledge needed to defend against ransomware.

INTERNATIONAL COOPERATION IN FIGHTING RANSOMWARE

Given the borderless nature of cybercrime, ransomware cannot be tackled by any single country alone. **International cooperation** is critical in tracking down and prosecuting ransomware operators, who often operate from regions with weak law enforcement.

Organizations such as **INTERPOL** and **Europol** are playing a pivotal role in facilitating cross-border cooperation. These agencies help coordinate international investigations, share intelligence, and bring together law enforcement from different countries to track ransomware groups and their infrastructure.

One notable example of international collaboration is **Operation GoldDust**, a global initiative led by Europol, which successfully brought down the REvil ransomware group. Through coordinated efforts across multiple countries, law enforcement agencies were able to dismantle REvil's infrastructure and arrest key members of the group, showcasing the power of international cooperation.

In addition to law enforcement, governments are forming **public-private partnerships** with cybersecurity companies and tech firms to enhance intelligence sharing and develop new tools to combat ransomware. These collaborations allow for the real-time exchange of threat information, which helps identify emerging threats before they cause widespread damage.

The Role of International Cybersecurity Regulations

As ransomware becomes an increasingly global issue, there is growing pressure for the development of **international cybersecurity standards** and regulations. Currently, different countries have varying levels of regulation and enforcement when it comes to cybercrime, creating gaps that ransomware operators can exploit. A global framework for cybersecurity would help close these gaps and ensure that all nations adopt minimum standards for protecting critical infrastructure and personal data.

One step toward such a framework is the **Paris Call for Trust and Security in Cyberspace**, a global initiative that promotes cooperation on cybersecurity issues, including ransomware. More than 70 countries, along with private companies and civil society organizations, have signed the Paris Call, committing to work together to address cyber threats.

THE FUTURE OF GLOBAL CYBER DEFENSE

Looking ahead, global efforts to combat ransomware will likely become more cohesive and sophisticated. As the threat grows, we can expect to see **greater harmonization of laws** across different jurisdictions, making it harder for ransomware operators to evade justice by moving between countries with lax cybercrime laws.

The use of **advanced technologies**, such as artificial intelligence and blockchain, will play a critical role in tracking ransomware payments, identifying criminal networks, and disrupting attacks before they reach their targets. Moreover, the continued rise of **cybersecurity insurance** will push businesses to adopt stronger defenses, as insurers demand that companies meet higher standards of protection to qualify for coverage.

International bodies such as the **United Nations** may also step up their involvement in combating ransomware, potentially leading to the creation of global cybercrime treaties and frameworks to govern cybersecurity practices.

FINAL THOUGHTS

Ransomware has rapidly become one of the most pervasive and destructive cyber threats of our time. Its evolution from basic malware to a sophisticated and targeted tool used by cybercriminals and, at times, nation-states, marks a dangerous new chapter in the world of cybersecurity. As we've explored throughout this book, ransomware doesn't just threaten individual users; it has the potential to cripple organizations, disrupt critical infrastructure, and endanger national security.

Understanding ransomware, from its origins to its modern-day iterations, is the first step toward effectively combating it. Armed with this knowledge, both individuals and organizations can adopt better defensive measures, remain vigilant, and minimize the risks of falling victim to these attacks.

The fight against ransomware is ongoing, and it will require continuous adaptation as cybercriminals refine their techniques. Governments, businesses, and individuals must remain proactive in their defense strategies, ensuring that they stay one step ahead of this evolving threat. The future may bring even more sophisticated forms of ransomware, but with global cooperation, technological innovation, and a commitment to cybersecurity, we can mitigate its impact and secure a safer digital environment for all.

GLOSSARY

- **Adware**: Software that automatically displays or downloads advertising content, often without the user's consent. While not always harmful, adware can sometimes come bundled with malicious software.
- **Artificial Intelligence (AI)**: The simulation of human intelligence by machines, especially computer systems, which can be applied to both attacking and defending against cyber threats like ransomware.
- **Backup**: The process of copying and storing data so that it can be recovered in case of hardware failure, data corruption, or cyberattacks like ransomware.
- **Blockchain**: A decentralized, digital ledger used to record transactions across multiple computers in such a way that the records cannot be altered retroactively, enhancing transparency and security.
- **Cryptocurrency**: A digital or virtual currency that uses cryptography for security. Bitcoin, Monero, and other cryptocurrencies are often used to pay ransom demands due to their anonymity.
- **Cyber Insurance**: A form of insurance designed to protect businesses and individuals from internet-based risks, including ransomware attacks.
- **Double Extortion**: A tactic used by ransomware attackers where, in addition to encrypting a victim's

data, they also threaten to release the stolen data publicly unless the ransom is paid.

- **Encryption**: The process of converting information or data into a code, especially to prevent unauthorized access. Ransomware typically uses strong encryption to lock files.
- **Europol**: The law enforcement agency of the European Union, which coordinates the investigation of serious international crimes, including ransomware attacks.
- **Exploit**: A vulnerability in software that cybercriminals can use to gain unauthorized access to a system or network.
- **General Data Protection Regulation (GDPR)**: A regulation in European Union law that governs data protection and privacy. Organizations must report breaches, including ransomware attacks, to authorities under GDPR.
- **Malware**: Malicious software designed to damage, disrupt, or gain unauthorized access to computer systems. Ransomware is a type of malware.
- **Phishing**: A form of social engineering attack where an attacker pretends to be a trusted entity to trick victims into providing sensitive information or downloading malicious files.
- **Ransomware**: A type of malware that encrypts a victim's data, rendering it unusable until a ransom is paid for its release, usually in cryptocurrency.

- **Ransomware-as-a-Service (RaaS)**: A business model where ransomware developers sell or lease their malicious software to less technically skilled criminals who then carry out attacks.
- **Social Engineering**: A technique used by cybercriminals to manipulate individuals into performing actions or divulging confidential information.
- **Spyware**: Malicious software that secretly records information about a user's activity on their device, often used to gather personal or financial information.
- **Trojan**: A type of malicious software that disguises itself as legitimate software, but once executed, allows attackers to gain unauthorized access to a system.
- **Worm**: A type of malware that can replicate itself and spread to other computers in a network without human interaction.
- **Zero Trust Architecture**: A security model that assumes no user, device, or network is trustworthy by default, requiring strict verification and continuous monitoring of all systems.

www.ingramcontent.com/pod-product-compliance
Lightning Source LLC
LaVergne TN
LVHW022005200926
848481LV00007B/2242
* 9 7 9 8 2 3 3 3 8 1 2 1 8 *